Estrella Polar

First edition: June 2015

www.estrellapolar.cat

ISBN: 978-84-9057-950-3
Legal deposit: B. 13.273-2015
Printed by SYL
Printed in Spain

TONI TERRADES ILLUSTRATED BY ÀLEX OMIST

THIS IS BARCELONA

Estrella Polar

So, you want to know more about Barcelona?
Well, you've got the right book in your hands!
To begin with, Barcelona is the capital of Catalonia and one of the most important cities on the Mediterranean, in Southern Europe.

Barcelona's history goes back many centuries. In Roman times, it was known as Barcino.

The city was founded by the Emperor Augustus, around the year 10 B.C.

In the Gothic Quarter there are still fragments of the old Roman wall that protected the city from outside enemies. This wall was 8 metres high and 2 metres wide.

Natives of Barcelona speak both Catalan and Spanish, and as in all big cities, many other languages can be heard in its streets.

Barcelona has nearly a million and a half inhabitants, distributed among ten districts.

Barcelona has four natural boundaries; the sea, the Collserola hills and the Besòs and Llobregat rivers. These geographical features provide reference points which help people find their way around the city and arrange places to meet their friends!

Most people prefer to move around underground, but there are also other interesting modes of transport... such as the tramvia blau!

There are 141 metro stations and during peak hours up to 134 trains run along the 102.6 kilometres of the network.

The city has not one, but two patron saints: Saint Eulalia and Our Lady of Mercy, or La Mercè as she is known locally.

September 24th is the day on which La Mercè, the most important festivity in the city's calendar, is celebrated. Year after year, these celebrations are plagued by wet weather.

Legend has it that the drops of rain are the tears of Saint Eulalia: she is upset that the city celebrates Our Lady of Mercy's name day more than it does hers.

La Mercè concludes with a big display of fireworks and music by the fountain at the foot of Montjuïc.

The Magic Fountain has become a symbol of Barcelona and is enjoyed by both locals and tourists.

Barcelona is on the coast and the city can get very humid. During the summer people like to swim in the Mediterranean to escape the heat.

Between the beaches of Sant Sebastià and Llevant, you can enjoy the popular resorts of la Mar Bella, el Somorrostro and la Barceloneta. The city has more than 4.5 kilometres of beaches.

The Canaletes fountain is a traditional meeting point at the top of la Rambla. It is also the place fans gather when FC Barcelona (Barça, as it is called locally,) win a trophy. According to legend, if you drink from this fountain you'll fall in love with Barcelona and will have no choice but to continually revisit the city.

The Boqueria Market was the first marketplace in Barcelona. Street vendors gathered here to sell meat as far back as the 13th century.

Nowadays you can also buy fresh fish, fruit, vegetables and all kinds of exotic products. The market is full of atmosphere, colours, tastes and aromas!

The Old Port, or Port Vell, is at the far end of La Rambla. From 1888 onwards it has been presided over by the famous statue of Christopher Columbus.

This statue serves as a lookout point from which you can discover a new perspective on the city from 60 metres in the air. If you want a different view, you can take a boat trip and admire the skyline of Barcelona from the sea!

Barcelona is a wonderful place to enjoy life on the streets. People spend a good deal of their free time on bar terraces. Whether they're talking business, chatting to friends, confiding in someone special or simply enjoying a moment of leisure, public spaces are full of people, day and night.

Plaça Reial in the Gothic Quarter is one of the liveliest squares in the city of Barcelona.

On the site of the old Roman Forum you will find Plaça Sant Jaume. This is the political centre of Catalonia and of Barcelona.

On one side of the square stands the Town Hall, on the other, the Palau de la Generalitat or Palace of the Catalan Government. Important decisions concerning the city and Catalonia are made in this square.

The 14th century saw an expansion of gothic splendour in Barcelona's architecture. Many important civil and religious buildings date from this period.

The church of Our Lady of the Sea, Santa Maria del Mar, is Barcelona's most treasured building in the Catalan Gothic style. The first stone was laid in 1329 and the church was completed in 1383.

The architecture of the Catalan Modernism movement is something of which the city is very proud.

Lluís Domènech i Montaner, Josep Puig i Cadafalch and Antoni Gaudí are the greatest examples of an architectural style which is admired and photographed by tourists from all around the world.

Passeig de Gràcia is the avenue that connects the city centre to the neighbourhood of Gràcia. It is also home to some famous buildings of Catalan Modernism. Situated near each other along the so-called «Block of Discord», they offer a masterly overview of these three Catalan architects.

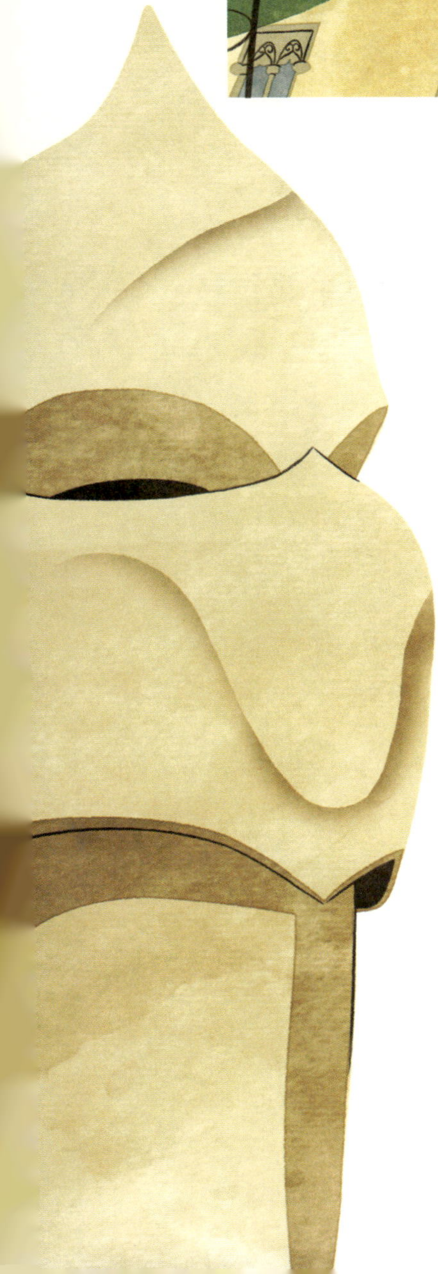

Passeig de Gràcia is also the most exclusive shopping strip in the city and an ideal spot to spend a lot of money. If you are short of cash you can practise the more affordable art of «window-shopping».

Opened in 1930, the Hospital of the Holy Cross and Saint Paul, (Hospital de la Santa Creu i Sant Pau) was designed by Domènech i Montaner. It provides another masterful example of Catalan Modernism in Barcelona.

This same architect is the author of yet another symbol of Barcelona and of Modernism: The Palau de la Música (Palace of Music). The unique stained-glass skylight in the ceiling represents the sun and allows natural light into the hall.

If there is one building, however, that everyone associates with Barcelona, it is the Sagrada Família.

The first stone of this temple was laid in 1882. Antoni Gaudí took over the project in 1883 and plans are it will be finished by 2026.

Do you want to see what the completed church will look like?

Barcelona is also the cradle of internationally-renowned artists. Geniuses like Picasso and Miró found great success in this city.

Not only did they live and paint here but they left permanent marks on Barcelona in the form of museums which bear their names and house important collections of their work.

In recent years the city has undergone a significant process of urban redevelopment.

The cityscape has been altered by contemporary architecture: the Agbar Tower by the Plaça de les Glòries, the Hotel Vela, on the seafront, and the MACBA building in the centre of the Raval neighbourhood are all good examples of this new, modern Barcelona.

Park Güell is another important manifestation of Catalan Modernism and unique in the city. The natural surroundings merge with the imaginative architectural elements and create a singular, fairy-tale atmosphere.

The Parc del Laberint d'Horta, which is the oldest public garden in Barcelona, and the Ciutadella Park are two more places you can visit if you enjoy relaxing or strolling leisurely in tranquil surroundings.

All kinds of animals can be found in Barcelona! The Zoo, opened in 1892, is home to lions, gorillas, hippopotamuses, elephants and hundreds of other species.

The Barcelona Aquarium offers a glimpse of life in the depths of the world's seas and oceans. You can spend hours here surrounded by colourful fish and enormous sharks.

TI
BI
DA
BO

On the Magic Mountain of Tibidabo, the highest peak in the Collserola hills which form the inland boundary of Barcelona, stands one of the oldest amusement parks in Europe.

This famous park was built in 1901 and offers spectacular panoramic views of the city.

The Hall of Mirrors, the Aeroplane, the Watchtower and the Museum of Automata are some of the oldest and most well-loved attractions in the park.

The residents of Barcelona love sports, particularly football. The home ground of FC Barcelona, called the Camp Nou, is one of the largest football stadiums in the world. Barça is internationally famous and is far and away the most popular football team in the city. However, a loyal minority support a second team, the RCD Espanyol.

RCD Espanyol, like Barça, has a historical link with the city of Barcelona. Supporters of Barça are referred to locally as culés, whereas fans of l'Espanyol are called periquitos, or parakeets.

In 1992, the eyes of the world were on Barcelona as it hosted the 25th Summer Olympic Games.

The Olympic Ring on Montjuïc is one of the large-scale redevelopment projects the city undertook in preparation for this important event.

Without doubt, Barcelona's current reputation as a modern international city dates from this intense period of modernisation and urban change.

404
812
1443
-2.0

This is Barcelona: a small metropolis sandwiched between the sea and the mountains and where, in the words of Miguel de Cervantes, everyone will feel welcome:

«Barcelona, the treasure-house of courtesy, haven of strangers, asylum of the poor, home of the valiant, champion of the wronged, pleasant exchange of firm friendships, and city unrivalled in site and beauty.» (Don Quixote de la Mancha, chapter LVXXII, translation by John Ormsby)

TONI TERRADES

THE AUTOR

has lived most of his life in Barcelona. He was born in Mallorca thirty-four years ago and studied Humanities. He's had many different jobs, mostly related to writing, translating and talking about books and writers. He combines these jobs with his activity as composer, singer and guitarist: he forms part of Bremen, a pop group with whom he has recorded a couple of albums...

ÀLEX OMIST

THE ILLUSTRATOR

was born in Barcelona forty-one years ago. Most of these he's spent drawing pictures. He used to draw everywhere and anywhere: during Physical Education classes, Philosophy lessons, even while he was watching Tom and Jerry cartoons, which is saying something! His parents, concerned for his future, enrolled him in a school of Art and Design. Nowadays he earns his living doing what he loves best: illustrating stories... anywhere and everywhere. He's even won some prizes, such as the Apel·les Mestre award for illustrated children's books.